START with a WORD

A JOURNAL for FINDING YOUR VOICE

GET YOUR PENCIL MOVING!

PETER H. REYNOLDS • ABRAMS NOTERIE, NEW YORK

Designer: Katie Benezra
Editor: Karrie Witkin
Production Manager: Rebecca Westall

ISBN: 978-1-4197-3829-6

Reynolds Studio assistance by Julia Anne Young

Peter Reynolds Font designed by Ana Parracho

Printed and bound in China
10 9 8 7 6 5 4 3 2 1

Abrams Noterie products are available at special discounts when purchased in quantity for premiums and promotions as well as fundraising or educational use. Special editions can also be created to specification. For details, contact specialsales@abramsbooks.com or the address below.

Abrams Noterie® is a registered trademark of Harry N. Abrams, Inc.

ABRAMS The Art of Books
195 Broadway, New York, NY 10007
abramsbooks.com

These words
belong to:

Words are . . .

WONDERFUL,
POWERFUL,
PERSUASIVE,
AND
BEAUTIFUL.

They are all around you, in books, on signs and posters, and in conversations.

YOUR BRAIN SOAKS THEM IN.

This journal is a place to catalog your words, collect new words, put them together in unexpected ways, and see where they take you.

May they spark new ideas, poems, and stories and ignite your passion for words!

Try to guess how many words you know:

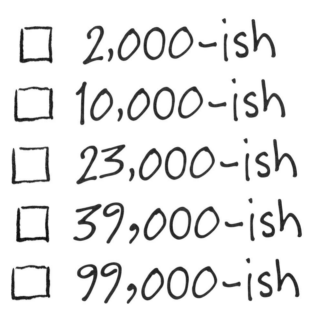

☐ 2,000-ish
☐ 10,000-ish
☐ 23,000-ish
☐ 39,000-ish
☐ 99,000-ish

According to studies, children know an average of 50 words by the time they are one, and about 10,000 words by the age of five. The average adult knows 25,000-40,000 words.

THINGS YOU'LL NEED:

DICTIONARY

PENCIL

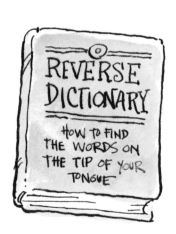

OTHER REFERENCES

THESAURUS

AND ERASER

(but it's better not to use
it too much—don't edit yourself!)

Start with one
of the most
familiar words you
know . . .

If you could change your name,
you would change it to:

If you wrote a book,
your pen name would be:

If you went undercover,
your alias would be:

Stuck? Try rearranging the letters in your
first and last names to make new ones.

Create an acrostic poem.

Write your name vertically on this page.
Then, write a poem in which each line begins
with a letter in your name.

You've been collecting
words since birth.

Do you know what
your first word was?

If so, jot it down.
If not, make it up!
Creativity and imagination are
encouraged in this journal.

Words help define
YOU.

Write down one of the
first words that comes to
mind to describe yourself.

Continue thinking about yourself. What other kind words come to mind?

me

Write about your earliest memories.

What words pop into your head when you recall your home? Your neighborhood? Your bedroom and toys? Your friends?

SUPERLATIVE WORDS

Let's jot down words that have
meaning in your life.

1 of your favorite books,
movies, or TV shows:

2 things you
are proud of:

3 of your biggest pet peeves:

4 places that make you happy:

5 things you'd grab if your house were on fire:

Do you have a favorite word?

No pressure. Come back to fill this in later, if you can't decide.

Keep a running list of other words that you love here.

TAKE A WORD
JOURNEY

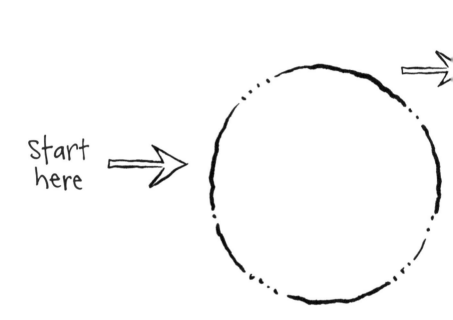

Start
here

End here!

Close your eyes. Open a book and place
your finger on a page. Write the word that
you are pointing to in the first bubble.

Then, fill in the next bubble with a word that
reminds you of that first word.

Keep free-associating
from one bubble to
the next, until all of
them are full.

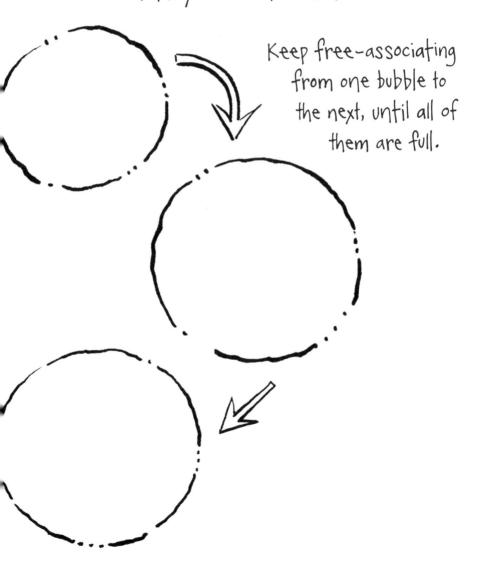

WORDS ARE PERSONAL

Home

Effort

Heartbreak

Kindness

Write down the words that come to mind
when you read each of the following . . .

Hope

Love

Loss

Happiness

WRITE
ONE WORD
THAT IS
ESPECIALLY
MEANINGFUL
FOR YOU.

Generosity.

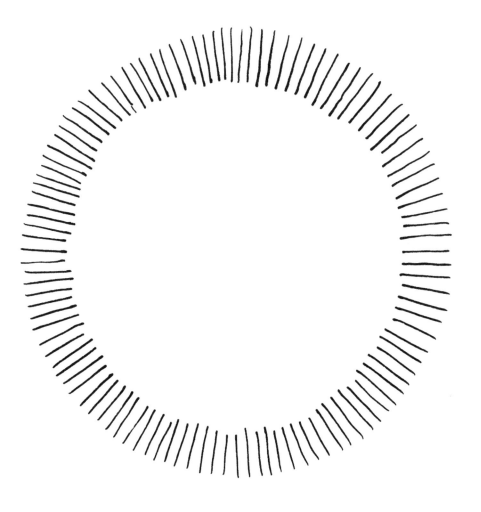

Relax . . . don't worry if this page stumps you.
Skip it and revisit it later when a word bubbles up!

WORLDLY WORDS

Maybe you speak more than one language.
Even if you are fluent in just one, you probably
know more words from other languages
than you might think! Jot some down here.

There are over 6,500
languages in the world!

MAGNIFIQUE!

 Open one of your favorite books.

Adjectives

1.

2.

3.

4.

5.

6.

7.

8.

9.

10.

Gather twenty random words (ten adjectives and ten nouns). Stay loose and don't put too much thought into it.

Nouns

1.

2.

3.

4.

5.

6.

7.

8.

9.

10.

Pick up a BOOK or MAGAZINE.

Take just ten minutes to scan it for words you don't know or that you are not quite sure about. Write them down here. It's wonderful to discover new words!

WORDS ARE COLORFUL

List a few words that you associate
with each of these colors.

Pink

Red

Orange

Yellow

Green

Blue

Purple

Black

Label these colors with new names.

POTATO PRAIRIE

MISTY MOSS

Pretend that you are the person responsible for naming paint samples or nail polish colors.

SEA DREAM

PERSIMMON POP

PICK YOUR
FAVORITE COLOR

Use it to write one of your
favorite words or a word
that reminds you of that color.

Add more swirls and
PIZZAZZ!

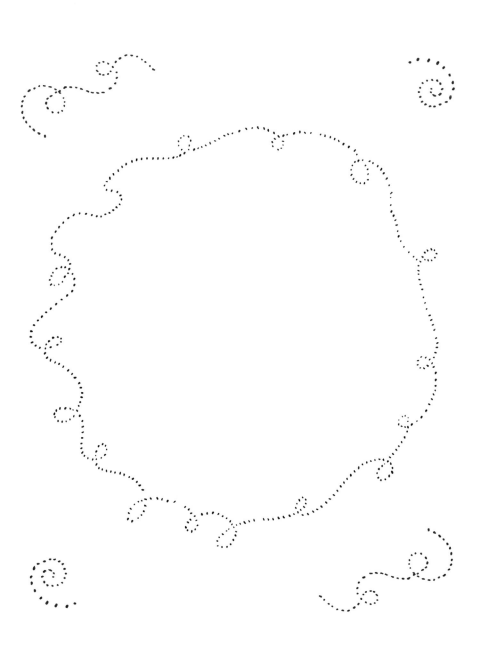

LISTEN
FOR WORDS

Watch a movie and jot down
words that jump out at you.

Write the first word that comes to mind for each letter of the alphabet.

A

B

C

D

E

F

G

H

I

J

K

L

M

N
O
P
Q
R
S
T
U
V
W
X
Y
Z

Write a poem, your thoughts, or a very short story sparked by these words:

BIG DECISION

WATCH FOR WORDS

Words are all around us.
We see them on billboards, packages,
trucks, buses, and more.

Be mindful. Seek them out.
Jot them down.

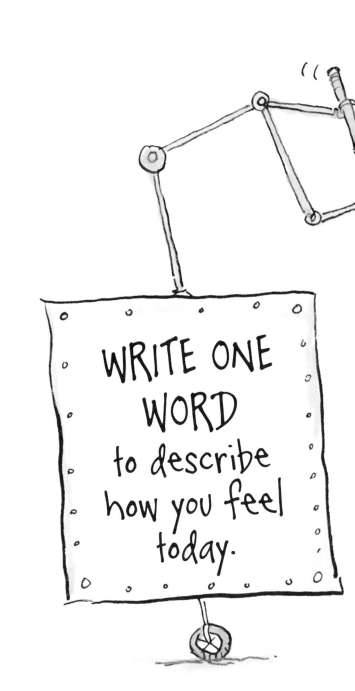

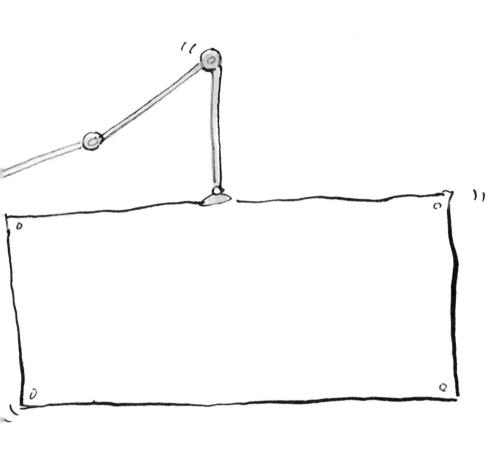

REINVENT THE QUOTIDIAN*

*Quotidian: occurring daily; ordinary or mundane

Make up new words
for the days of the week.

WHAT ELSE DO WE SAY EVERY DAY?

Write down
different words for

"HELLO"

and

"GOODBYE."

Invent a few new ones
if you want!

HELLO

_____

_____

_____

_____

_____

_____

GOODBYE

_____

_____

_____

_____

_____

_____

Howdy, Bagley!

Hello, Miss Rose!

NAMES BRING THINGS TO LIFE!

Imagine that ordinary things around you
become characters in a whimsical story.
Give each of these common items a fun name:

Chester Flanders

Knobby

McDreamy

Mervin

Your bed: _____

Your foot: _____

Your belly: _____

Your bedroom: _____

Your toothbrush: _____

Your breakfast: _____

Your dwelling: _____

Your pencil: _____

Your toilet: _____

Your socks: _____

NOW NAME THESE LIVELY CHARACTERS

GET TO KNOW
A WORD BETTER

Start with any word you've collected so
far or think of a favorite word
and write it here:

Look up your word in the dictionary
and copy the definition here:

Look up your word in a thesaurus and jot down
the synonyms and antonyms here:

Underline all the words on this page that appeal to you.
Discover any new ones?

NAME A BAND

Band names often use two or three
words that aren't typically put together.
Some examples: the Shrieking Librarians,
Volcano Kittens, and Astro Kale. Give it a try.
Who knows? One of these names might
inspire a story or a song!

MINDFUL WORDS

There are lots of words around
us, but there are words inside you too.
Close your eyes and sit quietly.

RELAX.

Listen to the words that emerge.
What words are floating around
in your head?

WORDS TAKE US PLACES

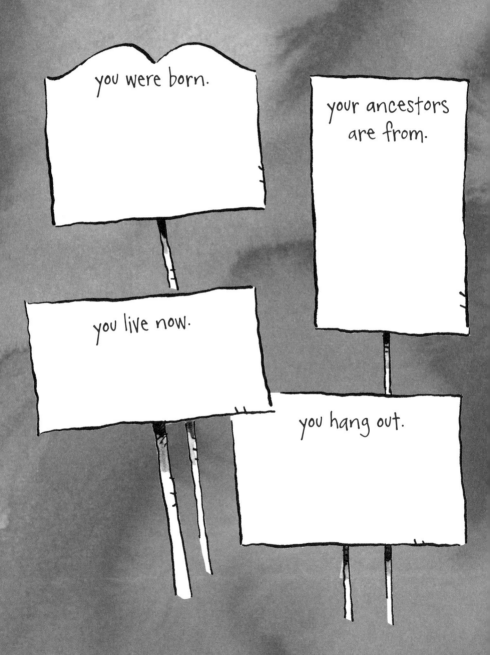

Think about the locations in your life.
Jot down the name of the place. . .

you
go to daily.

you traveled to
recently.

you want
to visit.

you want to avoid.

MAKE A MIND MAP

Start here

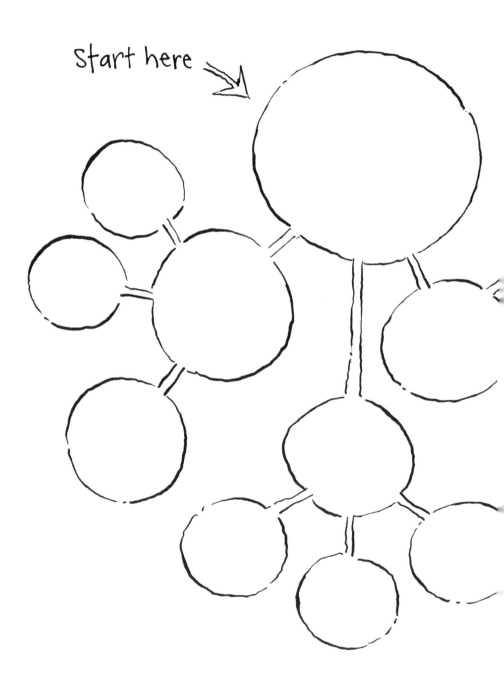

Start with the name of any place you love.
Then, fill in the next three bubbles with words you
associate with that place. After that, focus on
each of those three words and add more associations.
Stay loose! Keep going until all the bubbles are full.

INVENT A NAME
FOR YOUR HAPPY PLACE

If you'd like, look at your mind map
on the previous page for inspiration.

You can visit this place whenever
you want. Write the name here . . .

You've traveled deep into parts unknown and discovered some **WEIRD CREATURES.**

Give them names!

How much do you LOVE WORDS?

How Much I Love
Reading Words

○————————+————————————— Lov
              Like

How Much I Love
Writing Words

○————————+————————————— Lo
              Like

How Much I Love
Words in General

○————————+————————————— Lo
              Like

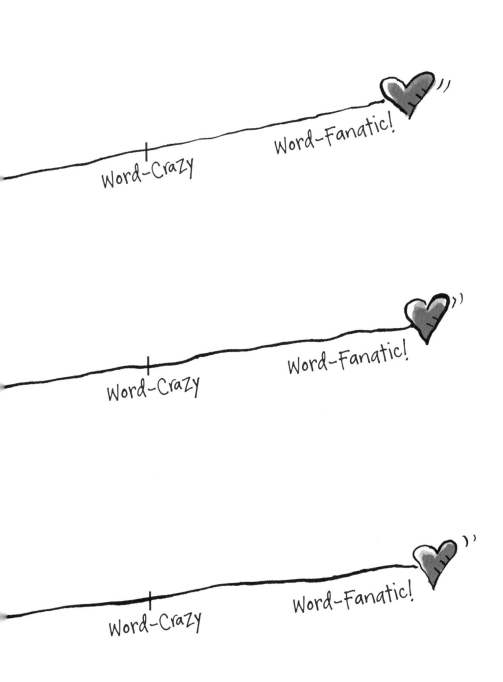

WORDS MAKE MUSIC

What is your favorite song?

Put on a random song and listen carefully. Write down the words that stand out to you here.

You could also keep a
list of some favorite
lyrics here too.

Some words imitate the sounds that they represent:

BUZZ

SIZZLE

BOOM!

HUH?

This kind of word is called an onomatopoeia.

Collect onomatopoeias here.

Some words sound just like their meanings.

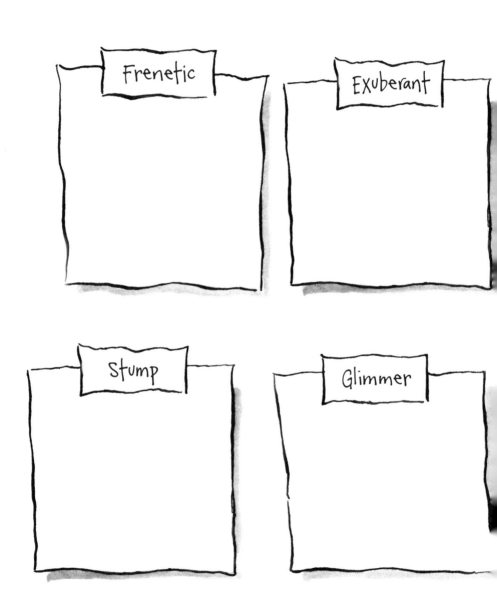

Frenetic

Exuberant

Stump

Glimmer

Draw an image for each of these words.

Frizzy

Sting

Wisp

Effervescent

TURN ON YOUR WORD RADAR

Pay attention to the conversations happening around you. Capture snippets of things that people say in the speech bubbles here.

WORDS ARE FUN TO SAY

They may sound beautiful even if you
don't know what they mean.
Keep a list of those words on the next page.

Words can be
MOUTHWATERING!

Make a grocery list that
includes all your favorite foods.

WORDS HAVE FLAVOR

A flavor or texture
(e.g., tangy, creamy)

1.

2.

3.

4.

5.

6.

7.

8.

9.

10.

They communicate the texture of food too. You can practically taste these words as you read them. Use this space to make three lists of words related to food.

A crunchy ingredient
(e.g., pretzel)

1.

2.

3.

4.

5.

6.

7.

8.

9.

10.

An ingredient you love
(e.g., chocolate)

1.

2.

3.

4.

5.

6.

7.

8.

9.

10.

MAKE UP NAMES

for the flavor combinations you like best! Draw ice cream cones too if you want.

SCENTS ARE POWERFUL

A certain smell can shift your state of mind or evoke a memory. Scents travel faster than language, but we use words to chase them! Collect your favorite smells in the bottles here.

TAKE A LONG,
DEEP BREATH.

What do you smell? Describe it
in as much detail as possible,
or identify it with just one word.

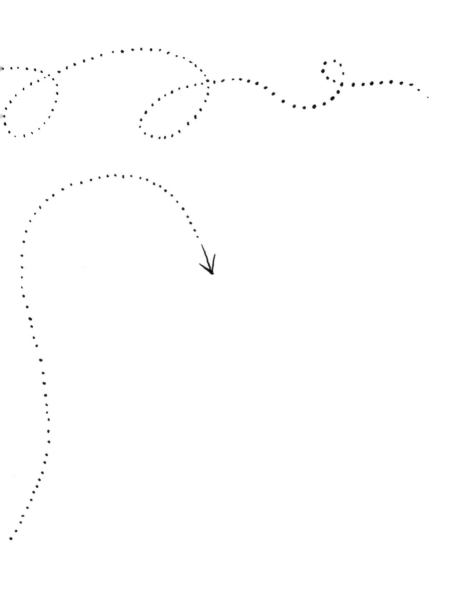

Words convey sensations!

FUZZY

SHINY

STICKY

SMOOTH

Free-associate with the words below. Jot down the first thing that comes to mind as you read each one.

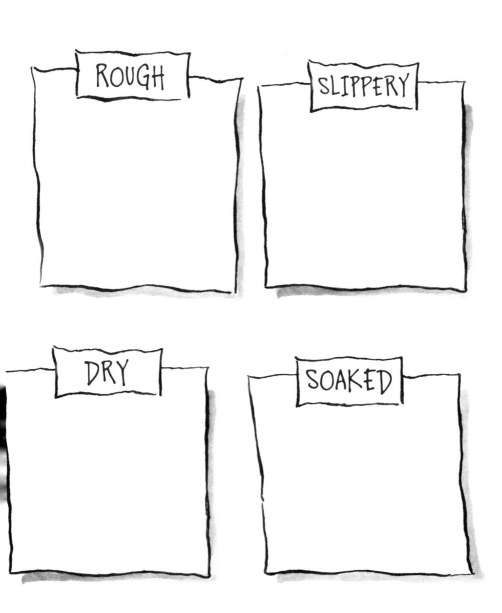

ROUGH

SLIPPERY

DRY

SOAKED

CHILL OUT

TRY THIS EXPERIMENT:
Sit in a quiet place and meditate on
words that you associate with cold things.
Do you feel yourself cooling down?

If you are already cold, try warming
yourself up by thinking about hot things!

COLD WORDS

Make lists of words that you associate with each season.

FALL

WINTER

WRITE A HAIKU ABOUT YOUR FAVORITE SEASON

A haiku is a style of poetry from Japan that has just three lines, consisting of seventeen syllables total. The first line is five syllables long, the second line is seven syllables long, and the third line is five syllables long. The lines do not rhyme (unless you want them to—bend the rules and have fun).

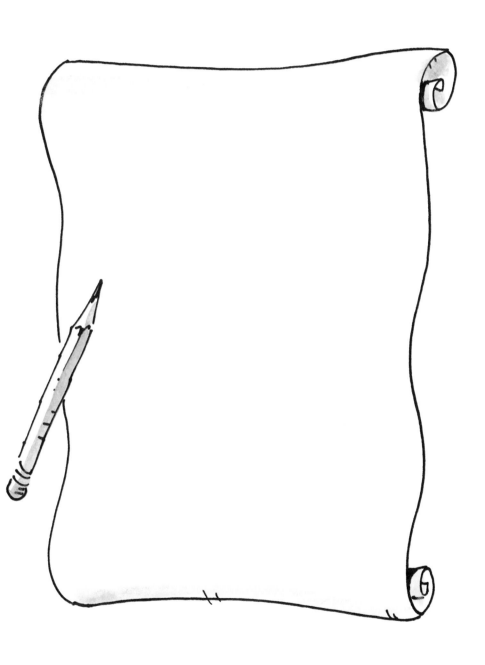

Fill the page with as many words as you
can think of to describe it.
How does this weather make you feel?

What is your favorite holiday?

Write about one particularly good holiday memory. Include colorful, flavorful, and sensory-filled words to bring that day to life.

COLOR IT WILD

List ten colors. Cover up that list and write a list of ten animals. Now uncover the color column to see how your words pair up.

COLOR

ANIMAL

1.

1.

2.

2.

3.

3.

4.

4.

5.

5.

6.

6.

7.

7.

8.

8.

9.

9.

10.

10.

Choose your favorite pairing from the opposite page. Write a poem or a short story about this creature (or doodle it if you'd like).

EDIBLE EMOTIONS

List ten moods. Cover up that list and make a list of ten foods. Now uncover the foods column and see what intriguing combinations you've cooked up!

MOODS	FOODS
1.	1.
2.	2.
3.	3.
4.	4.
5.	5.
6.	6.
7.	7.
8.	8.
9.	9.
10.	10.

Which word pairing represents something you'd most like to eat? Write a short story about what would happen if you did.

PREOCCUPATIONS

List ten adjectives. Cover up that list and make a list of ten professions. Now uncover the adjectives column and see if any crazy characters have emerged!

ADJECTIVES

1.
2.
3.
4.
5.
6.
7.
8.
9.
10.

PROFESSIONS

1.
2.
3.
4.
5.
6.
7.
8.
9.
10.

Choose one character from your lists and write a short story about a day in his or her life.

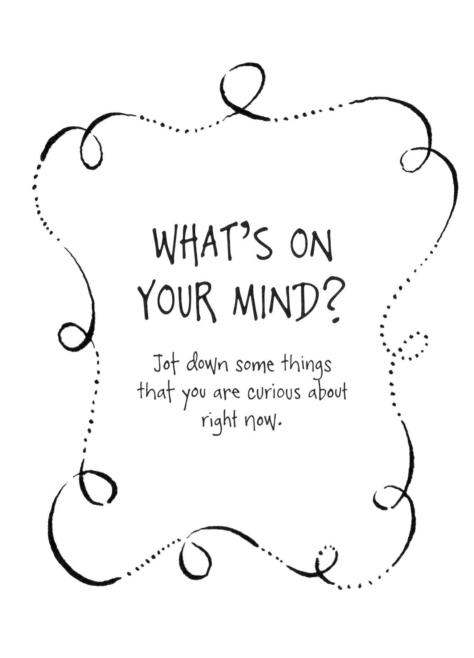

WHAT'S ON YOUR MIND?

Jot down some things that you are curious about right now.

CHOOSE ONE WORD

Write it over and over again. Write it as small as you can. Write it big. Write it backward. Try writing it upside down. In cursive. Mix print and cursive. Try different colors. A pen. A pencil. Fill these pages!

WORDS CAN BE CREEPY!

Especially when used in the right combination.

Look at the words below and write a few sentences or a poem using as many of them as possible.

COCKROACH	HUNGRY	LOCKED
MIDNIGHT	DRAFTY	SCRATCHING
ATTIC	SPIDER	DARKNESS
NIGHTMARE	RAT	SLIME
MONSTER	EARWAX	GHOST
BLACK CAT	SCAB	WITCH
SKELETON	CLOWN	HAUNTED

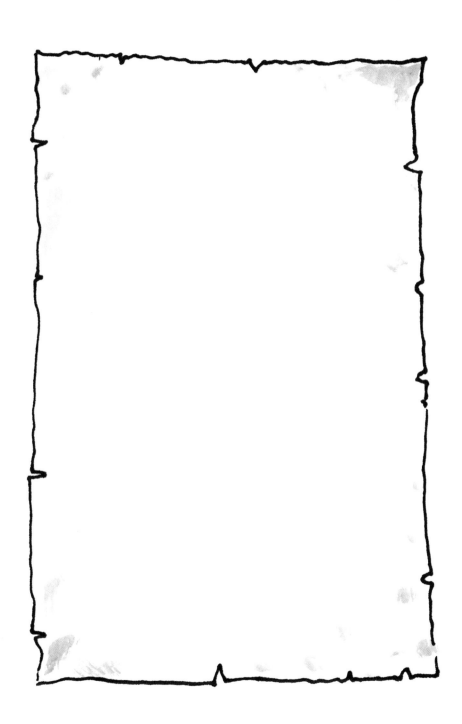

DO YOU HAVE ANY FEARS?

Give your fear a name. You could call it something ordinary, like "Charlie," or something elegant, like "Ophelia."

A name is a container. See if it contains your fear. Next time that feeling creeps up, you can say, "Oh, it's Ollie again."

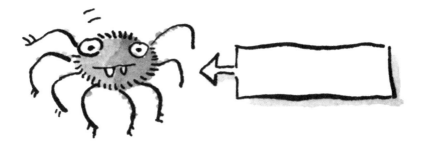

JOT DOWN YOUR FEARS:

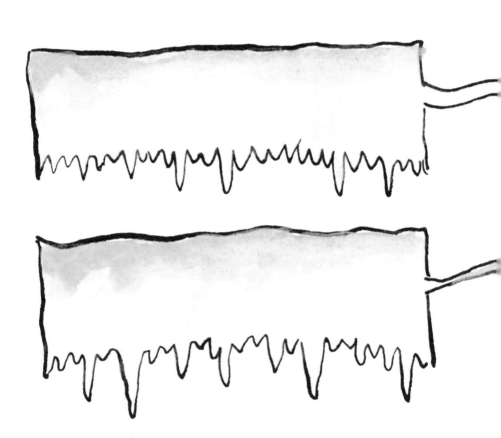

GIVE THEM NEW
NAMES HERE:

NOW WRITE ABOUT ONE FEAR,
referring to it by its new name.

WISH WORDS

What do you hope for and dream about?
Write it down in a few words. Putting your
hopes and dreams into written words gets you
one step closer to making them come true.

Tap your pencil
here three times
before writing for
good luck!

MINDFUL
WORDS

Jot down
one word that helps
your mind drift.

WORDS REMIND US OF PEOPLE

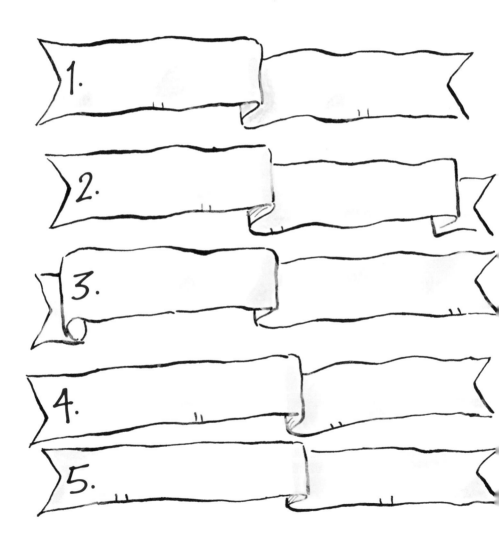

1.

2.

3.

4.

5.

Write down the names of ten people who are important to you, followed by the first word that comes to mind when you think of each.

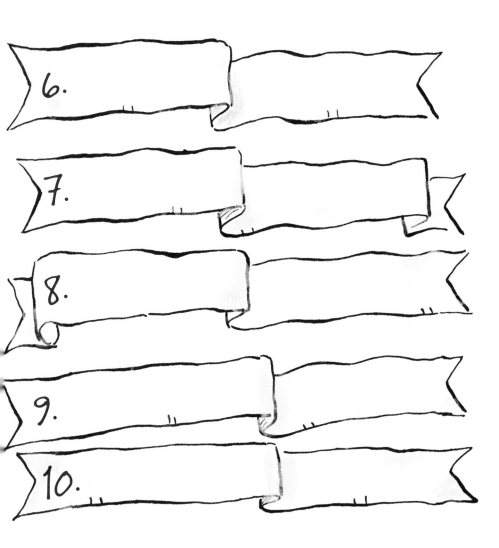

6.

7.

8.

9.

10.

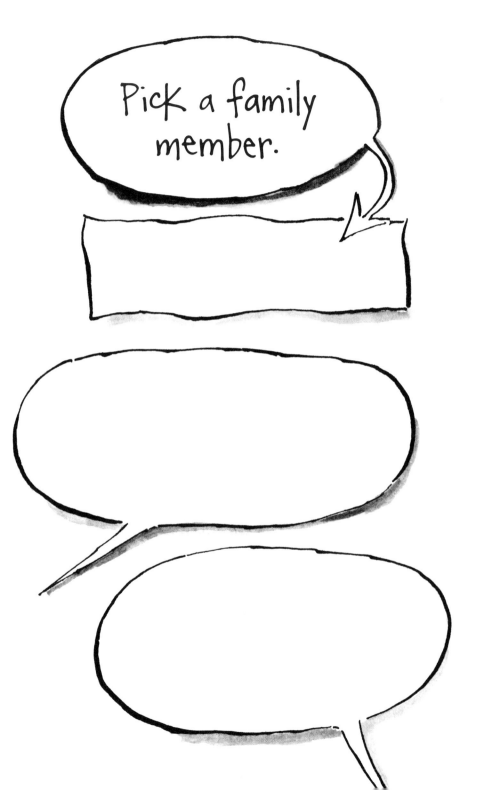

Jot down this person's favorite expressions and other words they frequently use.

WORDS
CONTAIN
WISDOM

Choose one person from your list
on the previous page and think about the
things you have learned from him or her.
Write a thank-you note here.

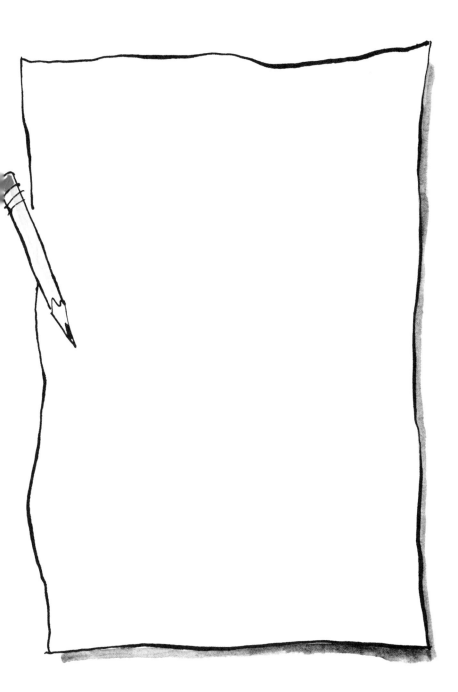

INVENT A SUPERHERO

EVERYDAY NAME:

SUPERHERO NAME:

SUPERPOWER:

WEAKNESS:

Think about the people in your life. What if their special qualities were enhanced and turned into superpowers? Pick one person and imagine their . . .

COSTUME:

VEHICLE:

ACCESSORIES:

SIDEKICK:

ARCHENEMY:

Capture it here, in one word . . .

Now invent a superhero persona for yourself.

EVERYDAY NAME:

SUPERHERO NAME:

SUPERPOWER:

WEAKNESS:

COSTUME:

VEHICLE:

ACCESSORIES:

SIDEKICK:

ARCHENEMY:

WHO IS YOUR HERO?

Pick one person living, dead, or fictional and write his or her name here.

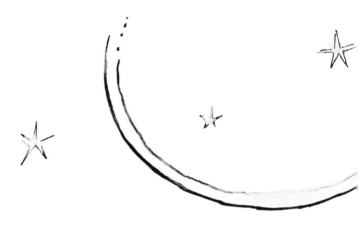

INTERVIEW YOUR HERO

Here are some questions you might ask...

When did you feel that first inkling of
what you wanted to do with your life?

_____

_____

_____

_____

What do you consider to be your
greatest accomplishment?

_____

_____

_____

What was the biggest challenge you faced?

_____

_____

_____

_____

Who or what helped you the most?

_____

_____

_____

_____

What did you have for breakfast?

_____

_____

SuperKowabungalotzafuzz!

Invent nonsense words!
Short ones. Long ones. Have fun!

Did you know that Dr. Seuss loved creating his own words?
ZAX. GA-FLUPPTED. SCHLOPP. DIFFENDOOFER.
ZIZZER-ZAZZER-ZUZZ. LORAX. Some of them have become
words we use often, like GRINCH and NERD.

WORDS NEEDED

Fill in the blanks with your own words.
Try some unexpected words. Drawing a blank?
Skip it and come back when you find
the word you were looking for!

1. The ship sailed _____.

2. It felt like _____ was
falling from the sky.

3. The alien emerged from the glowing spacecraft
and offered us _____.

4. I loved this day more than _____.

5. The moose hopped into the _____
and headed _____.

6. The King awoke to the sounds of a huge crowd chanting _____ .

7. Deepak's suitcase opened suddenly, spilling _____ all over the airport floor.

8. My wish came true. I awoke and there was _____ .

9. Penelope had discovered a new world after stepping through the portal. She decided to call it _____ .

10. _____ and _____ vowed to never _____ .

11. The _____ until one day _____ .

Here are NINE words with NINE letters.

Check off the words you already know
and jot down what they mean.
At some point, revisit this page to see
if you've learned any more of these words.
If you feel like it, look them up!

- [ ] SCHNOZZLE
- [ ] PAPARAZZI
- [ ] FLAPJACKS
- [ ] KRUMMHOLZ
- [ ] MEZZANINE
- [ ] QUIZZICAL
- [ ] PIZZICATO
- [ ] HARLEQUIN
- [ ] PACHYDERM

WORDS ARE INSPIRING

Use these pages to jot down your favorite quotes and phrases.

DON'T LET
NEW WORDS
ESCAPE YOU!

Keep hunting for words that
you don't know. Capture more
wonderful words here.

Keep Collecting WORDS.

Find the words you need
to express what is in
your head, your heart, your dreams.

May they help open
new doors to a stellar future!

onward